A Slippe

GW01465894

The Ordinatior
Homosexual Practice—a Case Study in
Biblical Interpretation

R T France

Formerly Principal, Wycliffe Hall, Oxford

GROVE BOOKS LIMITED
RIDLEY HALL RD CAMBRIDGE CB3 9HU

Contents

This booklet is a revised version of an essay published in a Festschrift for my friend Gordon Fee. The volume, edited by S V Soderlund and N T Wright, was entitled *Romans and the People of God: Essays in Honor of Gordon D Fee on the Occasion of his 65th Birthday*, and was published by Wm B Eerdmans in 1999. I am grateful to the publishers for permission to reuse the material in this form. As the title of the book indicates, the editors asked for essays to focus especially on Romans, and my essay was originally entitled 'From Romans to the Real World: Biblical Principles and Cultural Change in Relation to Homosexuality and the Ministry of Women.' In revising it for this publication I have not felt it necessary to remove the specific focus on Romans, since Romans 1.18–32 and Romans 16.1–16 would in any case play a significant role in my argument, and the comparison between the way these two passages function in this discussion provides an important illustration of the hermeneutical issues with which I am concerned. While some more personal observations appropriate to a Festschrift article have been eliminated, the remaining references to work by Gordon Fee are also relevant in this publication as he has in fact contributed in important ways to this debate.

The Cover Illustration is by Peter Ashton

First Impression June 2000
ISSN 1367–0840
ISBN 1 85174 434 7

1
Introduction

This booklet is about hermeneutics, how we get from an authoritative ancient text (the Bible) to practical decisions relating to the real world in which we live today. It aims to consider the tension which often arises between the desire to maintain biblical principles and the need to relate biblical values appropriately to a changing culture, and recognizes the sharply contrasting conclusions which can be drawn from the same biblical texts by interpreters who are equally eager to by guided by the authority of Scripture. I propose to examine the subject with reference to two of the most controversial areas in the Christian church in the Western world today, the issues respectively of homosexuality and of the ministry of women in the church.

The two issues are of course quite separate. Why then am I attempting to deal with them in a single study? In Britain, and more specifically in the Church of England, those who, like myself, have argued from Scripture for the appropriateness of ordaining women to positions of leadership in the church have often been confronted by others with the assertion that if our hermeneutical principles can lead us so clearly to discard the plain injunctions of Scripture on this one issue, we are bound also to approve homosexual practice, since the same principles apply.[1] This assertion is usually offered as a self-evident conclusion, if we are to be hermeneutically consistent. How can one with integrity adopt a 'liberal' position on the ordination of women and remain 'conservative' in relation to homosexual practice on the basis of Scripture?

In fact, however, while I do believe that it is right in the light of Scripture to ordain women to positions of leadership in the church, I cannot find similar scriptural warrant for approving homosexual practice. In other words, in my case the allegation that the same hermeneutical principles lead to a 'liberal' position on both issues is in fact simply not true. How then can I be so

---

1   Thus M Tinker, replying to an article by me on the ordination of women in *Churchman* 108 (1994) pp 234–241, writes: 'Formally the arguments and methodology used by Dr France in his paper are exactly the same as those used for legitimizing homosexual practice. Is it not time to question seriously an hermeneutic which leads to such results?' (*Churchman* 108, p 246). In remarkable contrast to this assessment, the 1997 consultation (in Kingston, Jamaica) of the Evangelical Fellowship in the Anglican Communion included the following words in its report: 'Attempts have been made to link the blessing of homosexual unions and ordination of practising homosexuals with the ordination of women in one agenda of "liberation." However, proposals for the ordination of practising homosexuals and for the blessing of homosexual unions attract two questions. Firstly, are homosexual acts sinful, forbidden by God? Secondly, if they are sinful, may the church formally bless and ordain people to live in unrepented and continuing sin? These questions have no parallel in the debate which surrounded the ordination of women. The state of being female is nowhere regarded in Scripture as sinful. The attempted linkage is disingenuous' (*Anvil* 14/3 [1997], p 217).

'inconsistent'? This has led me to examine again the hermeneutical basis for my conclusions on these two issues.

It so happens that Paul's letter to the Romans contains substantial passages which contribute significantly to the debate on each of these two issues. The total scriptural evidence is of course much wider in each case, but I hope that by discussing homosexual practice in the light of Romans 1.18–32 and the ordination of women in the light of Romans 16.1–16 we may uncover some useful hermeneutical pointers. The two passages are of course very different in character, but that is precisely the point. Not all of Scripture, even in Paul's letters, consists of specific injunctions or dogmatic propositions, and to take the authority of Scripture seriously means seeing all of it as (at least potentially) relevant for our guidance today. It should therefore be illuminating to explore how these two very different passages fit into the wider debate. If in the process we discover that within the compass of this one letter Paul appears to be, like me, 'conservative' in relation to homosexual practice and 'liberal' in relation to the ministry of women, I shall not wish to resist that conclusion!

2

Setting the Scene

I approach these issues in the context of the Church of England, which in 1994 for the first time ordained women to its priesthood, and in which there is at the time of writing a vigorous debate on the issue of homosexuality, with special reference to whether it is right for known practising homosexuals to be ordained.

Opposition to the ordination of women has come from two different quarters: from the catholic wing of the church mainly on the grounds that it is a departure from the tradition of the church (both Orthodox and Catholic); and from the evangelical wing on the quite different grounds that Scripture explicitly forbids women to have authority over or to teach men. The alliance of these two contrasting strands of opposition succeeded in preventing earlier attempts to have the measure approved by the General Synod, but in 1992 the necessary two-thirds majority was achieved with a number of evangelicals, who would previously have been expected to oppose the measure, now voting in favour. While it has been easy to caricature their change of mind as a capitulation to pressure from the church's leadership and/or an unprincipled bowing to secular culture, there has in fact been a significant hermeneutical reappraisal. What had appeared to be the 'plain teaching of Scripture' has been seen to be less one-sided than was previously thought. The division has been not on the basis of greater and less fidelity to Scripture, but rather on that of a genuine disagreement over how the varying strands of scriptural evidence relating to this issue should be applied to the current scene.

The resultant polarization of evangelical views has been an uncomfortable experience (though not a new one—evangelicals have seldom been a totally united body!). It has resulted in the setting up of the pressure group 'Reform,' dedicated to preventing any further erosion (as they see it) of traditionally-held evangelical positions. And many believe that the next step on the downward slope is likely to be the open recognition of homosexual practice as compatible with Christian discipleship, and therefore as acceptable in an ordained minister.

A few preliminary words of clarification of the issues involved may help to focus the following discussion.

The specific area of dispute with regard to women in the Church of England has been their ordination to the priesthood. For a good number of years women have been licensed as lay workers and as Readers, and since 1987 have been ordained as deacons. Evangelical Anglicans have, with few exceptions, been happy to welcome this extension of women's ministry. Ordination to the priesthood, however, has allowed women to fulfil certain additional functions (presiding at the eucharist, and the pronouncing of absolution and blessing), but more significantly from the evangelical point of view has opened the way to appointment as incumbent or priest-in-charge, and thus raises the question of a woman holding authority over men. It is here that some feel obliged to draw the line, on the grounds that 'Scripture forbids it.' The prospect before long of women becoming bishops clearly raises the issue of authority even more sharply.

With regard to homosexuality it is important to stress that what is under discussion is not homosexual orientation but homosexual practice. No doubt the distinction is over-simplified, but it marks a real difference of focus. The debate as to whether a homosexual orientation is innate or acquired will continue, and people will no doubt continue to be divided over these matters. But the issue from the point of view of scriptural authority is whether sexual activity between people of the same sex can be approved, and whether when such activity is acknowledged this should be regarded as a bar to ordained ministry.

With these broad definitions of the issues involved, we proceed to look from a hermeneutical point of view at each of the two questions in turn, before briefly comparing the two debates and drawing out the implications for biblical hermeneutics. In the space available all that can be offered is a broad-brush treatment, but I hope that its very lack of sophistication may make it easier to focus on the basic issues raised.

3

The Ordination of Women

I have recently discussed the hermeneutical issues relating to the question of women's ministry in the church in a series of lectures published under the title *Women in the Church's Ministry: A Test-case for Biblical Hermeneutics*.[2] Those lectures were specifically devoted to analysing why people have come to opposite conclusions in this debate, and to highlighting the hermeneutical issues raised. That book therefore covers the subject of this first main section of the present study more fully than is here possible, and I shall content myself with summarizing its argument, with the hope that any reader who wishes to explore the basis for the following remarks will be prepared to look up that fuller treatment (to which I have given some references in the footnotes).

i) The Shape of the Debate

Those who argue from Scripture that women should not be ordained usually rely on two separate but related lines of argument. The first is that there are two passages in Pauline letters which explicitly command women to be silent (1 Cor 14.34–35) and to refrain from teaching or having authority over men (1 Tim 2.11–12). The second is that in several places women are instructed to 'be in submission' (*hypotassomai*) to men. This injunction is explicit in Eph 5.22, Col 3.18, Tit 2.5, 1 Peter 3.1,5, and is also incorporated into the two texts just mentioned (1 Cor 14.34, 1 Tim 2.11). In one of these passages (Eph 5.23) Paul uses the metaphor 'head' to describe the relation of man to woman, and the same metaphor is used also in 1 Cor 11.3, though there without explicit use of the language of 'submission.'

To take the second line of argument first, there is no doubt that in the NT, and especially in Paul, there is a strong sense of a God-given 'order' in society and in the church, which includes the relationship of the sexes. What is not so clear is the sphere(s) of life to which this principle applies. Almost all the passages listed above use *hypotassomai* with specific reference to the marriage relationship, and it is at least arguable whether the principle may rightly be extended more generally to the relations of men and women in society or in the church. The ambiguity of the Greek terms *aner* (man *or* husband) and *gyne* (woman *or* wife) compounds the uncertainty. Where, as in most of the above passages, the writer is dealing specifically with marriage, the domestic

---

2   The Didsbury Lectures 1995, published by Paternoster Press, Carlisle, 1995, and by Eerdmans, Grand Rapids, 1997.

focus seems clear, but in 1 Corinthians 11.2–16 and 1 Timothy 2.9–15, passages which speak of church life, it remains to be decided whether Paul is speaking of a woman's silence and submission in relation to other men in general or only in relation to her husband.[3]

As for the metaphor 'head,' I am constantly amazed at the confident way in which people speak of a 'principle of headship' in the NT, apparently unaware that there is no such abstract noun ('headship') in the Greek NT, and that the noun 'head,' which is twice (and only twice) used metaphorically of man in relation to woman, is also used metaphorically of a variety of other relationships in ways which do not suggest a single unambiguous concept of 'headship.'[4] Moreover, one of the two metaphorical uses of 'head' for a man in relation to a woman (Eph 5.23) is explicitly concerned with the marriage relationship rather than with society in general. Clearly the metaphor must be understood in relation to its context; it does not in itself import a specific ideology.

Thus there is no doubt that the NT includes a principle of the 'submission' of woman to man (though also of mutual submission, Eph. 5.21), but there is room for considerable uncertainty about just what this 'submission' involves, and about how far it can legitimately be invoked outside the marriage relationship.

Paul and the Silencing of Women

Returning now to the other line of argument, the two Pauline 'prohibition texts,' we find that most of the discussion focuses on 1 Timothy 2.11–12. This is because everyone seems to find 1 Corinthians 14.34–35 hard to interpret in its context, and some doubt whether these verses, which seem awkwardly to interrupt the flow of Paul's thought, were originally a part of the letter.[5] Those who believe that Paul really did instruct the Corinthian women to be silent in church must also face the embarrassment that in 1 Corinthians 11.5 he accepts without comment that women were praying and prophesying in that same church. The fact that in 14.35 he goes on to mention specifi-

---

3   On the issue of submission and authority in this connection see further my *Women in the Church's Ministry*, pp 33–50.

4   1 Corinthians 11.3, one of the two places where 'head' is used as a metaphor for the relation of man (husband?) to woman (wife?), is especially interesting in that the same metaphor is used there also for the relationship between God and Christ, and between Christ and man. Clearly in all three cases it is a metaphor of priority in some sense, but the three relationships are different, and in the case of the God/Christ relationship a simple understanding of 'headship' in terms of authority and submission would have interesting trinitarian implications. Paul's choice of the 'head' metaphor in this passage is prompted by the issue of the covering of women's (literal) heads which it introduces; in vv 4–5 Paul may be deliberately playing on the ambiguity of the term when he speaks of 'dishonouring the head.' For a detailed discussion of 1 Cor 11.2–16 and its implications for the position of women today see G D Fee, *The First Epistle to the Corinthians* (Grand Rapids: Eerdmans, 1987) pp 491–530. More briefly see my *Women in the Church's Ministry*, pp 41–48.

5   *eg* G D Fee, *The First Epistle to the Corinthians*, pp 699–705.

cally their desire to ask questions, and instructs them to do so with their husbands at home, suggests to others that verse 34 was not in fact meant to be a blanket ban on all vocal activity by women in church, but rather a call for silence in certain particular circumstances, which seem to relate especially to married women. He has already issued such an injunction to tongue-speakers and prophets in verses 28 and 30 without suggesting that they be permanently silent.[6]

1 Timothy 2.11–12 thus remains as the one clear case of Paul's imposing a ban on women's ministry. There has been much debate on what sort of 'teaching' and 'authority' is involved, especially in view of the use of the rare verb *authenteo* rather than the normal language of authority (*exousia*),[7] and over whether here too *gyne* and *aner* refer specifically (and only?) to 'wife' and 'husband,' as may be suggested by the illustration drawn from the story of Adam and Eve (and finding the solution in childbirth) which follows in verses 13–15.[8]

But most interpreters have agreed that Paul (if we may assume that it *was* Paul: this is not the place to debate the authorship of the Pastoral Letters) does here prohibit teaching and authority for the women (or at least some women) of the church in Ephesus. Much energy has then been devoted to discerning whether this was the result of problems specific to that particular church at that time, or whether Paul might have been expected to say the same to women in other churches at other times as well. In particular much has been made of Paul's concern over apparently Gnostic teaching in the church in Ephesus, the instructions to Timothy to oppose those who devalue marriage, and the presence in that church of certain women who were going about 'saying what they should not say' (5.13).[9] On such grounds Gordon Fee has argued persuasively that the instructions in 2.11–12 relate to the specific local situation rather than laying down a universal rule, and that their status is comparable with that of the remarkably parallel rules for the treatment of widows in 5.11–15 of the same letter, which are not generally treated as normative for modern church life.[10]

The Wider Picture

Those who are unpersuaded that the matter is settled by these two traditional lines of argument (a general NT principle of female submission, and the presence of two passages prohibiting women's speaking/teaching/authority) typically respond by appealing to a wider pattern in the life and

6   On 1 Cor 14.34–35 see further my *Women in the Church's Ministry*, pp 53–56.
7   On *authenteo* see my *Women in the Church's Ministry*, pp 65–66.
8   On vv 13–15 see my *Women in the Church's Ministry*, pp 67–69.
9   On the special circumstances of Ephesus see my *Women in the Church's Ministry*, pp 57–62.
10 G D Fee, *Gospel and Spirit* (Peabody MA: Hendrickson, 1991) pp 52–65.

thought of the NT church. They point out Jesus' positive attitude towards women, particularly when seen against the background of contemporary Jewish and pagan attitudes. They note the prominent role which several women played in the life and ministry of the NT church, including in some cases apparently the holding of recognized offices in local congregations. Paul himself not infrequently refers appreciatively to the role of women whom he regards as in some sense colleagues in his gospel work, and in Galatians 3.28 famously declares that in Christ there is 'no longer male and female.' On such grounds they may speak of a development or 'trajectory' towards the elimination of discrimination between men and women in relation to Christian ministry which, even if not fully effective within the NT period, was inevitably destined to lead to women taking a full and leading role in the life of the churches. Some draw attention to the elimination of slavery as a parallel example of a trajectory which was set up in the NT but did not find its full outworking until many centuries later and in a different social and cultural context.

It is within this wider perspective that a remarkable passage in Romans comes into play, and it is to this that we now turn as the first of our two soundings in Romans.

ii) Romans 16.1–16

Nowhere else does Paul include such a long list of greetings in his letters. Perhaps it is because he is writing to a church which he has not yet visited that he feels it necessary to establish how many of its members he has already met and worked with on their travels in other parts of the empire. For whatever reason, he mentions no less than twenty-seven individuals in these verses, together with general greetings to the households of Aristobulus and of Narcissus. These twenty-seven are friends and in many cases explicitly designated as his co-workers. This passage therefore serves as a sort of roll-call of Paul's colleagues in ministry.

Its relevance to our present subject lies in the fact that ten of the twenty-seven people named are women. That in itself is remarkable in the context of what has often been assumed to be a predominantly male-led movement. It becomes the more remarkable when we note the expressions which Paul uses to describe a number of these women.

Four of them (Mary, v 6, Tryphaena, Tryphosa and Persis, v 12) are described as having 'worked hard.' The verb is *kopiao* and is used elsewhere of Paul's own apostolic ministry in evangelism and church building (for example in 1 Cor 15.10, Gal 4.11 and Phil 2.16) and of the parallel labours of his associates (1 Cor 16.16, 1 Thess 5.12). While the verb is not in itself very specific, the addition of 'in the Lord' with reference to the labours of Tryphaena, Tryphosa and Persis and of 'among you' with regard to Mary's work suggests that he refers to specifically Christian ministry. For some of the others the nature of that ministry is more explicit.

Prisca (v 3) and her husband Aquila are described as Paul's 'co-workers' (*synergoi*), the term he uses elsewhere for others who were his chief associates in his apostolic mission (Timothy, Titus, Mark, Luke, Philemon, etc). From other references to Prisca (= Priscilla), who is normally mentioned before her husband, we gain the impression of a woman with a significant and authoritative ministry, including the principal role in instructing the formidable Apollos in the faith (Acts 18.26)! Phoebe (vv 1–2) is a 'deacon' of the local church, which suggests a recognized ministry comparable to that of the deacons of Philippians 1.1 and 1 Timothy 3.8ff. She is also described by Paul as *prostatis* of himself and others, a term which is probably best translated as 'benefactor,' or perhaps 'patron,' and thus presumably a leading member of the congregation. But the most remarkable is Junia (v 7) who is described not only as Paul's 'fellow-prisoner' but also as 'prominent among the apostles.'[11] So do we have here a female 'apostle'?

The term 'apostle' is of course used of other Christian leaders of the first century besides the twelve and Paul (Acts 14.4, 14, 2 Cor 8.23 and elsewhere), but it is certainly a title of leadership. So Western Christians have tried to evade the force of Paul's language by turning Junia into a man, Junias. We cannot pursue the linguistic argument here;[12] suffice it to say that while the female name Junia is common, the supposed masculine form Junias occurs nowhere else in ancient Greek literature.[13] All the ancient translators and commentators on this text took Junia to be a woman. The first evidence for the name being taken as (masculine) Junias comes from the late thirteenth century, and in the East it was not until the nineteenth century that this idea emerged.[14]

The cumulative impression from Romans 16.1–16 is that Paul numbered women among his closest fellow-workers in his apostolic mission, that they held positions of recognized authority in his churches, and that they were engaged in teaching and indeed 'apostleship.' And Romans 16.1–16 does not stand alone—other references in Acts and in the other epistles reinforce

11   The rendering 'highly regarded *by* the apostles' has been suggested, but it may fairly be concluded that this unnatural reading derives not from linguistic probability but from apologetic embarrassment. It has not been adopted in any English version that I have seen.

12   C E B Cranfield, *The Epistle to the Romans* , vol 2 (ICC, T & T Clark, 1979) pp 788–789 is probably the best easily accessible discussion.

13   A remarkable example of masculine bias occurs in the Bauer lexicon on which students of NT Greek have been accustomed to rely. This lexicon, in its latest edition edited by Arndt, Gingrich and Danker, prefers the supposed masculine form Junias, admittedly 'not found elsewhere,' to the female name Junia (which it grudgingly admits 'from a purely lexical point of view deserves consideration') without pointing out that the latter is not only commonly found in Greek writings of the period, but is the unanimous interpretation of all ancient translators and commentators.

14   So K E Bailey, *Anvil* 11 (1994) pp 11–13.

this impression.[15]

All this seems to be in a different world from 1 Timothy 2.11–12, and to be hard to square with the belief that Paul's principle of female 'submission' extends outside the marriage relationship to include also the prohibition of authoritative ministry in the church. Could these verses have come from the same Paul who forbade the Ephesian women to teach or to have authority?

iii) Weighing the Evidence

The problem cannot be solved by arguing that either Romans 16.1–16 or 1 Timothy 2.11–12 was not written by Paul (there is scholarly support for either proposal)[16] since neither passage stands alone. They are merely prominent outcrops of two underlying strata in the NT, one restricting the role of women in at least certain spheres of church life, the other celebrating their role in ministry and leadership.

The interpreter is therefore left with a choice as to which of these two contrasting strands in the NT should take priority in drawing out guidance for modern church life. Hence the fundamental disagreement between equally sincere interpreters of Scripture over the ministry of women. It derives from opposite choices on this basic dilemma.

Some base their hermeneutic on the apparently clear 'prohibition' texts, understood in the light of a wide-ranging principle of male 'headship,' and so regard the prohibition as still valid for the church today. They must then deny that Paul's declaration 'no longer male and female' is relevant to ministry, and must find ways of reading texts like Romans 16.1–16 which maintain a distinction in principle between what women and men were allowed to do in the church.

For others the principle of 'no longer male and female' is fundamental, extending beyond simply the sphere of salvation to that of ministry in the church, and support for this is found in the NT evidence as to what women did in fact do (apparently with Paul's approval) in the first-century church. They must then question how widely Paul's principle of female submission can legitimately be extended, and must conclude that the prohibitions issued on women's activities in Corinth and Ephesus related to specific problems which had arisen in those particular situations. They will argue that the 'trajectory' of NT thought is clearly in the direction of greater equality between the sexes rather than towards a permanent male supremacy.

---

15 For comments on the role of women in the NT more generally see my *Women in the Church's Ministry*, pp 76–84. For a much fuller treatment see B Witherington, *Women in the Earliest Churches* (Cambridge: CUP, 1988).

16 Arguments for the non-Pauline authorship of the Pastoral Epistles are too well known to need documentation here. For the authenticity of Romans 16.1–16, see again Cranfield's commentary (*Romans*, vol 1 [1975], pp 5–11).

There seems no incontrovertible way of deciding which choice is right. Responsible hermeneutics is not an exact science, and equally convinced champions of the authority of Scripture for Christian life and thought today will no doubt continue to come to opposite conclusions in this area where each viewpoint can fairly claim to have Scripture on its side. While it may be 'obvious' to some which is the 'basic principle,'[17] the opposite may be equally 'obvious' to others.

The choice is often made not so much on the basis of an 'objective' hermeneutic as in the light of the tradition within which the interpreter has grown up and now operates. Change is also possible, however, as various outside influences are brought to bear and cause the interpreter to re-examine his or her hermeneutical assumptions. I have myself changed my mind on this issue, as had some of those evangelical Anglicans who voted in 1992 for the ordination of women (though I am not aware of many who have changed in the opposite direction). But in matters of religion change usually comes slowly, if at all! So, while both sides honour and wish to be guided by the same canon of Scripture, we must agree to differ.

---

17 *eg* F F Bruce, *Commentary on Galatians* (Exeter: Paternoster, 1982) p 190 (paragraph 3).

4
Homosexual Practice

The preceding section was a rather bald summary of an argument I have conducted in more detail elsewhere. Here I venture into what is for me new ground, at least in terms of any argument formulated for publication. If it appears at times to be simplistic, this is again due to the same constraint on space.

i) What Does Scripture Offer?

In the previous section I argued that the disagreement over the ordination of women arises from the fact that material can be found from Scripture in support of either viewpoint, leaving to the interpreter the ultimate decision on which takes priority. Is this the case also with regard to homosexual behaviour?

Biblical passages which refer directly to homosexual behaviour are not many, and all can be briefly mentioned here.

In the OT there are two stories of attempted homosexual rape (Gen 19.1–11, Jdg 19.22–30), each of which serves as the trigger for severe punishment whether by God (Sodom) or by his people (Gibeah). In each case there was also a flagrant breach of the laws of hospitality, but from the way the story is told it is clear that the attempted sexual assault is the focus of judgment. But these are accounts not of homosexual behaviour as such, but of attempted abuse and violence. To argue from these passages for a prohibition of any homosexual activity would be as irresponsible as to conclude from the condemnation of heterosexual rape that any intercourse between men and women is forbidden. They give no encouragement to loving homosexual behaviour, but neither do they directly condemn it.[18]

More relevant are two passages in the law which prohibit male homosexual practice ('lie with a male as with a woman') and declare it to be an 'abomination' (Lev 18.22, 20.13). These passages, brief and undeveloped as they are, are quite unequivocal. They occur in the setting of other laws against sexual misconduct such as adultery, incest and bestiality, listed as the sort of behaviour for which the pagan nations have been driven out of the land.

---

18 The reference in Jude 7 to the sin of Sodom and Gomorrah as 'indulging in immorality and [literally] going off after other flesh' reflects the story of attempted homosexual rape in Genesis 19, and is widely assumed to locate the sin of the men of Sodom particularly in their homosexual inclination. Some commentators argue, however, that it refers rather to their desire for sexual relations with *angels*: so *eg* R J Bauckham, *Jude, 2 Peter* (Word Biblical Commentary, Waco: Word, 1983) p 54. 'Other flesh' would be a strange term for fellow-men. The passage is too obscure to be used confidently on either side of this debate.

The penalty in Leviticus 18 is to be 'cut off from their people' (v 29) and in Leviticus 20 is death.[19]

Deuteronomy 23.17–18 prohibits Israelites from being male prostitutes, and declares their earnings 'abhorrent to the Lord your God.' The Book of Kings condemns the presence of male prostitutes in Judah, as an aspect of pagan worship, and an offence in the sight of God (1 Kings 14.24, 15.12, 22.46, 2 Kings 23.7). Again, as with the stories of attempted homosexual rape, we must beware of equating prostitution with homosexual activity in general, but it seems clear that the homosexual activity involved in male prostitution was not acceptable and was particularly associated with pagan worship.

In the NT we find similarly brief and undeveloped condemnations of homosexual behaviour in 1 Corinthians 6.9–10 and 1 Timothy 1.9–10. In the former passage *malakoi* and *arsenokoitai* are among the immoral people who will not inherit the kingdom of God, while in the latter *arsenokoitai* are among a similar list of unrighteous practices (including also parricide, murder and slave-trading) which are 'contrary to sound teaching.' While there is room for debate over the meaning of *malakos* ('soft,' 'effeminate,' but sometimes used more specifically of the younger partner in a pederastic relationship, or a male prostitute),[20] there seems little doubt that *arsenokoitai* ('those who go to bed with males,' echoing the terms of LXX Lev 18.22) in both passages is intended to cover male homosexual activity in general rather than only pederasty or male prostitution (for each of which more specific Greek words were available).[21]

And those few passages, apart from Romans 1.18–32, to which we shall turn shortly, are all that can be reasonably claimed as direct reference to homosexual activity in the Bible. It is, it will be noticed, uniformly hostile. These few references must, moreover, be set alongside the underlying biblical assumption from Genesis 2.24 onwards that God's purpose for human sexuality is to be found in the heterosexual union of man and woman. The fact that so few references to homosexuality occur suggests perhaps not that the matter was of little consequence, but that homosexual behaviour, so common in the pagan world of both Old and New Testaments, was simply alien to the Jewish and Christian ethos.

Where then can those who wish to argue on biblical grounds for the legitimacy of homosexual activity turn for support? They can of course attempt to deflect the negative verdict drawn from the above passages by arguing that they refer not to loving homosexual relations but to perversions

---

19 A further law in Deut 22.5 condemns transvestism as 'abhorrent to the Lord,' but without exploring the motive behind it; this law may relate to homosexual activity, but the background is obscure.
20 G D Fee, *The First Epistle to the Corinthians* pp 243–4.
21 See the full study of the word by D F Wright, *Vigiliae Christianae* 38 (1984) pp 123–153.

such as pederasty, prostitution and rape. In the absence of more detailed description in the relevant passages this is a hazardous enterprise, even though the very brevity of the references perhaps leaves scope for constructing such an argument (essentially an argument from silence) for each passage taken alone. But in view of the overall negativity of these passages taken together such an attempt is not likely to convince in the absence of any overt encouragement to homosexual love to counterbalance these references. Can any such encouragement be found in the Bible?

Appeal is made in this connection particularly to the love of David and Jonathan. Jonathan 'loved David as his own soul' (1 Sam 18.1–4), 'as he loved his own life' (1 Sam 20.17); they wept and kissed each other at their parting (1 Sam 20.41); and David declared Jonathan's love for him 'wonderful, passing the love of women' (2 Sam 1.26). There is, however, no indication of any sexual activity between them (kissing between men was common, as it is in many cultures today, and had no necessary sexual connotations). Their 'love' was a firm, loyal and unselfish friendship, expressed in a 'covenant' (1 Sam 18.3; 20.8, 16–17, 42) which led Jonathan to prefer David's interests to his own. It is perhaps not surprising that the strong emotional language (and especially the phrase 'passing the love of women') has been taken in our culture to suggest something more sexually expressed, but this remains speculation, and speculation which finds no support in the general pattern of sexual relations in Israel as far as we can discern it from the OT. The stories of David's family and sexual affairs provide ample evidence of his heterosexual orientation!

The fact that Jesus was, as far as we know, unmarried (and that celibacy was unusual in Jewish culture) has led some to speculate that he was homosexual in orientation. His selection of an all-male group of disciples can be no cause for surprise in the culture of his day, but one of them is singled out in the Fourth Gospel as the disciple 'whom Jesus loved,' and this close relationship (including his reclining at the Last Supper 'on Jesus' chest,' Jn 13.23, 25) has led some to suggest that he was not only a specially close friend but a sexual partner. We are again confronted by the difficulty of deciding what would be the force of such expressions in a cultural context different from our own, but here too it must be insisted that no hint of sexual interest, let alone sexual activity, is found in the Gospel text.[22] Only a culture which has difficulty in appreciating close friendship between men on any other basis

22 The expression 'reclining on the chest of' is rightly translated by modern versions by some such phrase as 'reclining next to,' indicating the position to Jesus' right at a formal meal (using something like the Roman *triclinium* arrangement, where guests reclined at table supported by their left elbow).

would think of importing a sexual element into this language.[23]

But if there is no evidence of approved homosexual activity in the Bible, might it be possible to argue for it on more general grounds of a Christian ideal of love and acceptance and of the tolerance of differing views within the church (as in Romans 14), together with the fact that cultural attitudes have changed, and that these ideals must now be expressed in a way appropriate to our culture, even if it would have been unacceptable in that of the Bible? Does cultural relativity allow us to condone or even promote what the biblical writers condemned? It seems that this must ultimately be the basis for an attempt to provide scriptural support for homosexual behaviour, and to this proposal we shall return in our final section.

ii) Romans 1.18–32

Other biblical references to homosexuality are, as we have seen, very meagre. But here is a passage which not only offers a more explicit description of homosexual behaviour, but also sets it deliberately in a theological context. This, therefore, has rightly become the central passage in any discussion of biblical teaching on homosexuality.

The passage as a whole is a denunciation of human 'ungodliness and unrighteousness.' It forms the first element in Paul's cumulative argument that 'the whole world is held accountable to God' (3.19), since 'both Jews and Greeks are under the power of sin' (3.9). In 1.18–32 the focus is on Gentile sinfulness, before turning to the Jews especially in chapters 2 and 3.

The essence of Gentile sin is their refusal of the evidence of creation and their consequent idolatry, worshipping the creature rather than the Creator (vv 18–23). Homosexuality is brought into the argument to show the result of the essentially perverted orientation expressed in idolatry. It is one of the vices to which in consequence 'God gave them up.' Many other aspects of sinful behaviour are listed in vv 29–31, but it is their sexual activity which is picked out for special condemnation.

In v 24 there is a broad statement about their 'uncleanness and dishonouring their bodies among themselves,' which is not expressed in specifically homosexual terms. But in vv 26–27 Paul is quite explicit. The terms he uses are heavily loaded ('natural'/'unnatural'; 'burning with desire for each other'; 'committing shameless acts'; 'due penalty for their error'), but his target cannot be mistaken. He is describing same-sex sexual activity, and uniquely in the Bible he specifies female as well as male homoerotic behaviour. There is no qualification in terms of whether the relationship is one of

---

23 One might compare the persistent tendency in later Christian legend, still exploited by some 'sensational' modern authors, to portray Mary of Magdala as Jesus' sexual companion. Here too the driving force is not anything in the biblical text but a culture which demands a (in this case heterosexual) 'romantic element.'

love and consent or of exploitation and violence. It is the 'unnatural' sexual activity which is itself the evidence of the 'God-forsaken' state of such people, and of their liability to God's wrath. They know that such behaviour deserves death, yet they not only practise but even applaud it (v 32).

The total condemnation of homosexual behaviour seems inescapable. And Paul clearly feels strongly about it. How then can those who wish to claim that homosexual activity is compatible with biblical values evade the force of this passage? One strategy is to regard the passage as no longer ethically relevant: it is simply an expression of the limited outlook of Jews and Christians in biblical times which must now be set aside in favour of a proper expression of Christian love and tolerance in a culturally altered world. We shall return to this argument shortly. But is there anything in the passage itself which may give us pause? Two aspects of the passage have been appealed to.

One is the observation that this is a Jew writing about Graeco-Roman culture. The language of these verses reflects a conventional Jewish critique of pagan idolatry and ethics.[24] But what was abhorrent to Jewish thought (as the few OT references noted above indicate) was widely accepted and prized in the Graeco-Roman world. Homosexual partnerships, whether pederastic or between adults, are accepted without comment, and described with appreciation, across a wide range of Greek literature. What to the Jew was 'unnatural' and repulsive was to the Greek noble and praiseworthy. Paul, as a Jew, simply did not understand, and what we find in Romans 1.26–27 is merely Jewish cultural prejudice.

Such an argument raises in an acute form the issue of biblical authority. The Bible message is encapsulated in a specific culture, and the attempt to extricate it is hazardous, especially when, as in this case, a substantive Bible passage is not merely sidelined but declared to be quite wrong. If we were dealing with a passing illustration, this might seem less drastic (though it would still raise important questions about where the authority is located); but this is an essential plank in Paul's central theological argument, presented in detail and with passion. Jew or not, he writes as God's apostle and with deliberate emphasis. If *this* passage can be set aside on the grounds that its author was Jewish, what other part of the Bible is safe?

The second argument against accepting this passage as a total ban on homosexual activity for Christians focuses on Paul's use of the terms 'natural' and 'unnatural.' On this view 'unnatural' sexual acts are indeed to be condemned, but for the true homosexual homoerotic behaviour is entirely

---

24 *cf* Wisdom 14.12–31, which includes in v 26, among many other evil results of idolatry, *geneseos enallage* (NRSV, NEB 'sexual perversion'; NJB 'sins against nature') which means literally something like 'inversion of generation' (so *Jerusalem Bible* notes); in Rom 1.26 Paul uses cognate language when he speaks of 'exchanging' (*metallasso*) natural sex for unnatural.

natural. Indeed for someone of such orientation to attempt heterosexual intercourse would be 'unnatural,' and it would be this rather than their homosexual behaviour which would properly incur the condemnation of this passage.

Paul is not speaking, however, about the 'nature' of an individual, which may differ from that of another.[25] Rather *physis* refers to 'nature' in general, the established order of God's creation. Paul uses the same term of the laws of horticulture in Rom 11.24 and of the difference between the sexes in 1 Cor 11.14. *Physis* in these passages seems to mean something like 'the pattern of God's created world,' 'the way things ought to be.' Homosexuality, on this understanding, runs counter to the way God has designed human sexuality. It is thus in essence a misuse of God's creation, whatever the personal inclinations of an individual.[26]

iii) Toward a Biblical Understanding of Homosexuality

On the issue of the ordination of women we came to the conclusion that each side in the current debate could find relevant scriptural support, and that in the end it comes to a decision as to which strand of biblical evidence should take priority. In such a situation those who claim to be subject to the authority of Scripture may justly conclude that the 'innovation' of ordaining women is a proper outworking of biblical principles, even though they would be unwise to claim that their position is the only one which is open to an honest evangelical, or to echo the celebrated assertion of the Archbishop of Canterbury that opposition to the ordination of women is a 'heresy.' The question which now confronts us is whether there is a comparable choice to be made with regard to the acceptance of homosexual practice. Does the Bible here also leave us with a dilemma?

Wolfhart Pannenberg answers that question decisively: 'The Bible's assessments of homosexual practice are unambiguous in their pointed rejection, and all its statements on this subject agree without exception.'[27] Our survey of the biblical material above supports his conclusion, which has also been the overwhelming tradition of Christian teaching through the ages. The situation is thus decisively different from that with regard to the ministry of women. On homosexual practice the Bible speaks with a consistent voice.

---

25 See M Vasey, *Strangers and Friends* (London: Hodder & Stoughton, 1995) p 131.
26 The overall tenor of the passage in relation to homosexual practice is well summarized by J D G Dunn, *Romans 1–8* (Word Biblical Commentary, Dallas: Word, 1988) pp 73–74.
27 Taken from a brief summary article published in the *Church Times* of 21st June 1996, under the title '*Amor vincit omnia*—or does it?' Pannenberg concludes that a church which 'ceased to treat homosexual activity as a departure from the biblical norm...would stand no longer on biblical ground but against the unequivocal witness of Scripture' and 'would thereby have ceased to be one, holy, catholic, and apostolic'!

Christian arguments in favour of homosexual practice have therefore not surprisingly tended not to focus much on Scripture. There have been attempts, as we have noted above, to suggest that one or another biblical passage does not mean what it has generally been understood to mean. But more often the argument has been that the biblical condemnation of homosexual practice, clear as it is for its own day, does not apply to ours. For some this view may take the form of a simple rejection of any authority for the Bible in deciding on contemporary issues: to appeal to the Bible at all is an anachronism.

Cultural Change and the Primacy of Love

But if we want to take the authority of the Bible seriously, we do not have the luxury of such a simple cutting of the hermeneutical knot. There are two main lines of defence against this apparently total biblical condemnation, which reinforce one another. One is to argue that the cultural change has been so great that the sort of homosexual practice promoted today is quite different from that which the Bible writers attacked. The other is to apply to this issue more general biblical principles of love and tolerance which, while admittedly not applied to this issue within the Bible, may nonetheless be felt to be relevant to it.

The former view, that loving homosexual relationships as we know them today are in principle quite different from what the Bible writers condemned, suggests that modern studies of homosexuality have invalidated ancient understanding of it. They have certainly introduced new terminology, and have put the whole issue on a more sophisticated basis of experimental evidence and of psychological explanation (though their conclusions in these areas are far from unanimous). But it is not true that the ancient world knew nothing of loving homosexual relationships, even if it may have lacked the scientific expertise to interpret them as we would. The approval of homosexual feelings and behaviour in the Graeco-Roman world was based on the view that, where not abused, they are good and loving. They were not regarded as in themselves 'perverted.' And Paul, as a well-educated Hellenistic Jew from Asia Minor, could not have been unaware of this evaluation among his Greek fellow-citizens, which is well known to any classical scholar. If Paul then chose to bracket all homosexual acts together as 'against nature,' it was not because he was unaware of a less negative view, but because he deliberately chose to oppose it. He is not an innocent abroad, but a clear-sighted and radical critic of an aspect of local culture which he knew well, but believed to be incompatible with the purpose of God for his creation.

The appeal to the primacy of love in this connection may seem to take us straight back to the ethical debates of the sixties, and in particular to the contention of 'Situation Ethics' that the principle of love overrides moral rules. Here it was argued that whatever in a given situation is perceived to be the most loving course is right, even if it may run counter to sexual or other rules (such as the prohibition of adultery) which have traditionally been derived from the Bible. We need not return to that debate; suffice it to say that the main stream of Christian ethical thinking has not been convinced that moral rules are so easily discarded, and has found it more appropriate to speak of the rules as a vehicle of love rather than as its opposite.

This is not to devalue the primacy of love, but to argue that its primacy does not leave it as the *only* relevant ethical principle. The real world is not so simple, and moral choices are regularly made in situations where biblical principles are found to be in tension with one another and to point in differing directions. In such cases 'love' may often be the arbiter, though to determine what is the most loving course can be an extremely subjective decision. But the biblical material relating to homosexuality does not seem to admit of such arbitration. When all the specific material relevant to the issue in Scripture seems to point in the same direction, have we the right to define 'love' in such a way as to overturn that consistent witness?

It is important to recognize that the biblical witness to which I refer is not only the handful of 'negative' texts we have looked at above, but also (a) the absence of any 'positive' texts on the subject, and, more importantly, (b) the general tenor of biblical teaching and example which indicates that God has designed human nature for heterosexual love and intercourse. It is against this consistent background that the negative references to homosexual behaviour find their proper place.

Ultimately, then, we must decide what are the acceptable limits of the argument from cultural change. Social conventions are different in our day from biblical times, and homosexual behaviour has achieved greater social acceptance in modern Western society than it has ever known before within the Judaeo-Christian tradition. In such a situation is it appropriate to apply the great biblical principles of love and tolerance to this particular aspect of human choice even though it would have been unthinkable so to apply it within the cultural context of first century Christianity? If in this case the principle of love appears to be in tension with the Bible's heterosexual understanding of God's purpose, may the latter legitimately be subordinated to the former?

Or is it after all possible to uphold the biblical sexual ethic without thereby forfeiting the claims of love towards the homosexual? Can love coexist with ethical disapproval? I hope it will be clear from the above that I believe that it can and should, and that a responsible understanding of the authority of the Bible for ethics cannot afford to discard the Bible's consistent witness on this controversial issue.

5
Conclusion

In attempting to be guided by the Bible we find (even within the constraints of space of this booklet) a significantly different situation with regard to the ordination of women from that with regard to homosexuality. In the former we are confronted with a tension between two strands of biblical material which appear to lead us in different directions. In such a situation we cannot escape the need to make a decision as to which of these strands should be regarded as expressing the more fundamental principle, and should therefore take priority in formulating a biblical attitude for today. But in the case of homosexual behaviour there seems to be no such divergence in the biblical witness, and so no comparable hermeneutical decision to be made. There is instead a consistent, if limited, pattern of biblical teaching and example which indicates that homosexual activity, however loving and well-motivated, is not in accordance with God's design for his human creation.

Biblical Principles in a Changing Culture
Why then is it suggested, as we noted at the beginning, that the same hermeneutical principles govern the two issues, and that those who conclude that women should be ordained to positions of leadership in the church are bound also to conclude in favour of homosexual activity? The suspicion here is that on both issues a vote for change from what has been the traditional Christian position is simply a capitulation to the 'spirit of the age,' a weak acquiescence with the strident propaganda of the feminist and homosexual lobbies, and an unwillingness to risk being seen as 'negative' and 'old-fashioned' by upholding biblical standards.

No hermeneutical activity takes place in a cultural or historical vacuum. The history of biblical interpretation is the story of new insights discovered often under the pressure of changing circumstances and of cultural shift— the eventual abolition of slavery is a celebrated example. The increased recognition of the 'positive' strand in biblical thinking about the ministry of women has undoubtedly been triggered by wider debate about the place of women in society, and the recognition that a church which refused to ordain women was finding itself increasingly out on a limb and subject to misunderstanding and abuse from a more 'liberal' culture. But it has been the result not of apologetically discarding the biblical witness, but of re-examining it in the light of the changing agenda and of discovering there things which we had not previously sufficiently noticed.

But to re-examine our position in the light of the secular agenda is not necessarily to change it. In the case of the role of women it has indeed led many of us to change, because, we believe, a balanced understanding of the Bible itself demands it. But in the case of homosexuality the re-examination of the Bible has not had the same result. Rather it has led us to re-affirm the traditional Christian view, because we find that this is what the Bible supports, and further study has served only to reinforce that conviction.

The Obvious and the Incidental

Our study has focused particularly on two passages from Paul's letter to the Romans. On each of the two issues studied Romans offers a passage which contributes significantly to the debate. But the two passages are very different, and to reflect on their different character and their place in the discussion may prove interesting from the point of view of hermeneutical method.

With regard to homosexuality, Romans 1.18–32 includes the most prominent biblical treatment of the subject, not at a narrative level but as a matter of theological reflection. Paul states his position forcefully and unambiguously, and his statement is agreed on all sides to provide a fundamental plank in constructing a biblical approach to the issue, whether the interpreter is sympathetic to Paul's expressed viewpoint or not.

With regard to the ministry of women, however, Paul makes no pronouncement on the subject in this epistle. What we find instead is an intriguing insight, apparently almost accidental, into Pauline church practice in the listing of some of Paul's fellow-workers in Romans 16.1–16. It might then be objected that this passage is not suitable for use in trying to resolve a controversial issue in the way that Romans 1.18–32 is. Surely we should base our biblical principles on the overt theological pronouncements of the biblical writers, not on such *obiter dicta*.

But it is my contention that a truly biblical hermeneutic must not confine itself to the overt pronouncements of the apostolic writers, but must be open to the biblical evidence as a whole, including its narrative and incidental parts. When this broader approach is undertaken, it may lead us to re-examine the way we have understood some of the more 'obvious' texts. If it is the case that Paul approved and valued the ministry of women alongside men in the way that Romans 16.1–16 reveals (and there is plenty of evidence elsewhere in the NT to support this conclusion), this poses important questions about our interpretation of the texts which have traditionally been supposed to prohibit any such activity on the part of women. If the Paul who wrote 1 Corinthians 14.34–35 and 1 Timothy 2.11–12 also wrote Romans 16.1–16 (and indeed 1 Cor 11.1–16), it is *prima facie* unlikely that he really meant that no woman must ever speak or exercise authoritative ministry in the church.

Thus alongside the deliberate pronouncements of Romans 1.18–32, the 'incidental' evidence of Romans 16.1–16 also has a vital, though different, role in a truly biblical hermeneutic. If this recognition makes the task of deriving guidance for the real world from the biblical text more complex than it might at first have seemed, so be it. Let us hope that by embracing the wider range of biblical evidence we are enabled to be more responsible in offering biblical guidance for the issues of our generation.